ADRIANISMS

THE COLLECTED
WIT AND WISDOM
OF ADRIAN ROGERS

Innovo Publishing LLC
www.innovopublishing.com
1-888-546-2111

Providing Full-Service Publishing Services for
Christian Authors, Artists, and Organizations: Hardbacks, Paperbacks,
eBooks, Audiobooks, Music, and Film

ADRIANISMS

The Collected Wit and Wisdom of Adrian Rogers

This book contains quotes and statements of Dr. Adrian P. Rogers during the tenure of his pastoral ministry. While the quotes and statements are literal quotes and statements of Dr. Rogers, the publishers disclaim that they are all original with him and may contain statements that, in whole or part, were previously or first stated by others.

Library of Congress Control Number: 2015944158
ISBN 13: 978-1-61314-286-8

Interior Layout & Cover Design by Innovo Publishing LLC

Printed in the United States of America
U.S. Printing History
First Edition: August 2015

CONTENTS

Preface V

The Character of God 9

The Lordship of Christ 37

The Word of God 55

Prayer 77

The Fruit of the Spirit 93

Growing in Grace 101

Victorious Living 129

A Word to the Wise 151

Relationships 179

Encouragement 195

Sin and Temptation 219

Truth 255

The Church 265

Money 279

Just for Fun 289

Heaven 307

Preachers and Preaching 313

Prophecy 323

Salvation 331

Adages and Axioms 359

PREFACE

If you've ever heard a message by Adrian Rogers, then you are keenly aware of his quick wit. He was always ready with a quip, an anecdote, or a whimsical poem. He loved alliterations, and certainly could turn a phrase with the best of them. He was a master of the language. His wit was disarming, and it was endearing.

Yet in addition to his wit, Adrian Rogers also possessed exceptional wisdom. He had a way of taking common things and saying them in such an uncommon way so as to make you think through them all over again. And conversely, he could take uncommon things and put them in unusually common terms.

But neither his wit nor his wisdom ever overpowered the message of the Gospel; rather, it complemented it—just little snippets sprinkled in to season the message. They were a tool—a gift—he used to effectively tell others of Jesus, to break down barriers, to bring the point from an intellectual level to a personal one, and to diffuse even the most antagonistic arguments.

While many of the remarks are entirely original and were coined by Adrian Rogers, he was also widely read and picked up countless sayings, expressions, and stories from others' writings. He gathered rhymes, jingles, and expressions from as far back as childhood, and it appears he never forgot a single one. It would be impossible for us to trace all of these back to their sources, so we readily admit that although many are not original, they were appreciated by Dr. Rogers and employed in his own unique way. Over the years they have become identifiable with, almost inseparable from, him. They have become "Adrianisms."

In a very real sense, the collection of Adrianisms is all about the future, because it represents the powerful teaching being broadcast every day to you and others literally around the world over the Love Worth Finding program. This ministry is still changing lives because our commitment is to proclaim "the unsearchable riches of Christ" (Ephesians 3:8) that never changes.

And now we invite you to enjoy the wit and the wisdom of Adrian Rogers.

ADRIANISMS

THE COLLECTED
WIT AND WISDOM
OF ADRIAN ROGERS

CHAPTER ONE

THE CHARACTER OF GOD

God is Love,
Jesus is Wonderful.

Try to define the Trinity and you'll lose your *mind*.
Deny it and you'll lose your *soul*.

*D*on't rest in your salvation experience.
It is the Christ of your experience
that keeps you.

God is never late or never in a hurry.

God is *not* some cosmic kill-joy.
Every time He says, "Thou shalt not,"
He's simply saying,
"Don't hurt yourself."
And every time He says, "Thou shalt," He's saying,
"Help yourself to happiness."

God only wants for us
what we would want for ourselves
if we were *smart enough* to want it.

God the Father is all there is.
The Holy Spirit is all we will feel.
And Jesus is all we will ever see.

Has it ever occurred to you
that *nothing*
ever occurs to God?

If I had a **thousand** lives to live,
I'd give **every one** to Jesus.

I love the name of *Jesus*.

It fits just right on my tongue.

I love Jesus with every nerve, every fiber, and
every sinew of my being.

I am

the visible part of the invisible Christ.

He is

the invisible part of the visible me.

If Jesus doesn't *excite* you,
maybe you have
calluses on your soul.

God grades on the cross,
not the curve.

Our God is a God of second chances.

The difference between the Anti-Christ and Christ is that one gives me a number and the other gives me a name. When Jesus comes, will my name be called or will my number be up?

What we need is not great faith
but faith in a great God.

Believe in *miracles* but trust in *Jesus*.

There is no promise God cannot keep,

no prayer God will not answer,

and no problem too hard for Him to solve.

Christianity is not a code,

a cause, or a creed,

but Christ.

Everything *over* my head
is *under* God's feet.

God doesn't

just love *all* of us.

He loves *each* of us.

Our great need is to discover that
Jesus is all we need.

To **KNOW** Him is to love Him.

To **LOVE** Him is to trust Him.

To **TRUST** Him is to obey Him.

And to **OBEY** Him is to be blessed by Him.

Even when you don't *feel* loved,

God loves you.

It's not Jesus and—

or Jesus or—

It's Jesus ONLY!

Don't ask God to cram His plan into your puny little mind because then God would be limited by your understanding.

Jesus is our way to God
and God's way to us.

How come you're always running around

looking for God?

He's not lost.

Jesus became forever like me

that I might become forever like Him.

I can preach truth,
but only the Holy Spirit
can impart truth.

God is sovereign,
so live confidently.

God is holy,
so live reverently.

God had much rather
forgive
than He had to
judge.

I have been selected by the *Father*,

saved by the *Son*,

and sealed by the *Spirit*.

On Creation:

The closer you look,

the more you see God.

If you **bargain with God,**
you **cheat yourself.**

God doesn't love us
because we're valuable.
We're valuable
because God loves us.

*W*ith God, a few will do.

Bethlehem—God with us.
Calvary—God for us.
Pentecost—God in us.

Heaven
is all that the loving *heart* of God
would desire,
the omniscient *mind* of God
can conceive,
and the omnipotent *hand* of God
can perform.

God is willing to
accept the responsibility
for a life dedicated to Him.

Everything God does is wonderful...
until we get used to it.

God has no draftees,
only *volunteers.*

If you feel far away
from God,

guess **who** moved?

*G*od is
searching our hearts
in order to
supply our deepest need.

God is waiting for *me*

to wait for *Him*.

God is the Inventor.
Man only discovers *God's*
many wonderful inventions!

God is America's biggest threat
and our only hope.

God isn't your *Father*
just because
He is your *Creator.*

I am God's melody of life,

and He sings His song through me.

God makes me want to work,
and then *He* does it for me.

He became
as I am
so that I might become
as He is.

God's **two greatest gifts** are

Jesus

and

time.

*I*f God wanted to prove Himself, He could
roll back the heavens and make Himself
known with a display of His grandeur,
might, and glory. However, such displays
would render faith unnecessary.

Men throw broken things away,
but it seems God never uses anything until
He first breaks it.

Now go home
and put your head upon
your pillow and

sleep well,

for He that watcheth
over Israel
shall neither
slumber nor sleep.

I have never known a time
when God was not
totally sufficient.

God will never do for us what we
could and *should*
do for ourselves.

The doctrine of the
Trinity
is not beyond
logic and reason—
just *above* it.

Stop telling God how big your storm is.
Instead,
tell the storm how big your God is.

Thank God for the
mystery of the manger,
the blessings of Bethlehem,
and the treasures of the Trinity.

The Holy Spirit is to a Christian
what instinct is to an animal.

The *Holy Spirit*
leads you,
but He never
drives you.

The great God of the universe
Who heaped up the mountains,
scooped out the oceans, and flung out the stars
wants to have a relationship with
you.

The Holy Spirit
never leaves a *surrendered* vessel
unfilled or unused.

We can *never* really go

where God is not;

and where He is,

all is well.

*W*hen we start to take credit

for what **God** does,

then He stops doing it.

Where God doesn't rule,

He will

overrule.

With God,

timing

is more important than

time.

You will never learn that
God is all you need until
He is all you have.

You don't have to know
why
when you know
Who.

THE *L*ORDSHIP OF *C*HRIST

*I*f Christ is not
Lord of all,
He's not
Lord at all.

Fear of God is love on its knees.

God doesn't want *a place in your life.* He
demands and deserves preeminence.
God's throne is not a duplex.

If Christ is worth anything,
He's worth everything.

If He is not your Lord,
He is not your Savior.

If I put *things* between me and Christ, it is idolatry.

If I put *Christ* between me and things, it is victory!

Christianity is not a cafeteria line where you say,

"I'll have a little salvation

but no Lordship right now."

You'll never be over those things

that God has put under you

until you are under those things

that God has set over you.

$\mathcal{A}$uthority and submission
are two sides
of the same coin.

$\mathcal{B}$eing baptized with the Holy Spirit means He is now Resident in your heart. Being filled with the Holy Spirit means He is now President there.

He died to *claim* me as Lord.

He lives to *control* me as Lord.

$\mathcal{M}$ost people want to serve God
but only in an advisory capacity.

My fear of God should not be
that He will put His hand on me
but that He will take it off.

No matter how wise or capable you are, before
you leave the harbor, you'd better make certain the
Captain is on board.

The first mark of a man made new is that
he is under new management.

❧

There's only one alternative to obedience to Christ,
and that's disobedience.

❧

Until you know the restraint OF THE SPIRIT,
you'll never know the release OF THE SPIRIT.

When you turn away
>from the knowledge of God,
>>that is a matter of faith.

When you turn away
>from the authority of God,
>>that is a matter of love.

*W*hatever master a man chooses
will master that man.

You don't make Him Lord.
He's Lord already.
You just recognize it.

No man can serve two masters,
but he must serve one.

The devil has more power than I do,
but I have more authority.

The one who fears God the most
loves God the best.

The Christ-filled life
is a **self-emptied** life.

CHRIST + I AM NOTHING = CHRISTIAN

Two words that will change your life:
"Yes, Lord."

We shouldn't surrender to preach, teach, or do anything.
We should surrender to God.

When Saul met Jesus, he asked the two greatest
questions anyone could ever ask:
"Who are You, Lord?"
and
"Lord, what do You want me to do?"

WHAT we surrender, God takes.
WHAT He takes, He cleanses.
WHAT He cleanses, He fills.
WHAT He fills, He uses.

Adrianisms

You don't have to know when, where, or why.
Just know Jesus and move when He moves.

You can't just
tip your hat
to Jesus;
you must
bow your knee.

He being infinite
suffered in a finite period of time
what we being finite
would have suffered in an infinite period
of time.

Everybody needs a

hero.

Jesus is mine.

I may know Him better,
but there's nothing
better than knowing Him.

If Jesus Christ is still in that grave
nothing really matters,
but if He came out of that grave,
nothing but that really
matters.

If you read the **Bible** and you don't find Jesus,
go back and reread it.
It is a **"Him-book."**

$\mathcal{I}$s Jesus boring?
Are you hemmed in by Jesus?
That's like a minnow
hemmed in by the Atlantic Ocean.

Jesus didn't practice
what He preached.

He preached
what He practiced.

When Jesus did *miracles*,
they were
not publicity stunts.

Jesus came
to reveal
the character of God,
not to display
the grandeur of God.

Jesus gave Himself for me,
so He could give Himself to me,
so He could live His life through me.

When we see Jesus, I believe we will say,

"What questions?"

Jesus was as much man
                 as if He weren't God
and as much God
                 as if He weren't man.

There is no security in heaven.
The security is in Jesus.

Jesus sees through us,
and He sees us
through.

Let the presence of Jesus guide you.

Let the promises of Jesus gladden you.

Let the power of Jesus guard you.

You can try to block out the
Light,
but you cannot put it out.

It doesn't matter
what you are right about
if you are wrong about Jesus.

You are on Jesus' prayer list.
The Lord Jesus knows you by name,
and He calls you by name.

CHAPTER THREE

THE WORD OF GOD

I read other books;
the Bible
reads me.

To understand the part of the Bible
you don't understand
is to obey the part you do understand,
and before long you'll begin to understand
what you didn't understand.
Understand?

The weakest ink is better
than the best memory.
Study with pen in hand.

If you have a Bible that's falling apart,
you'll have a life that's not.

This book will keep you from sin, or sin will keep you from this book.

—Dwight L. Moody

Receive the Word of God with a *reflective* spirit:

- Is there a promise to claim?
- Is there a lesson to learn?
- Is there a blessing to enjoy?
- Is there a command to obey?
- Is there a sin to avoid?
- Is there a new thought to carry with me?

The Bible is God's love letter to His children.
If you don't understand it, it's because you're reading
someone else's mail.

The Bible addresses
one problem—sin.

The Bible has
one villain—Satan.

The Bible has
one hero—Jesus.

The Bible has
one purpose—to glorify God.

The Bible is not the book of the week;
it is not the book of the month;
nor is it the book of the year.
It is the *book of the ages!*

The Scriptures are shallow enough
for a babe to come and drink
without fear of drowning
and deep enough
for theologians to swim in
without ever reaching the bottom.

—St. Jerome

$\mathcal{T}$he Word of God is to your spirit

what **blood** is to your body.

When asked to **compromise** in order to bring
peace to the Southern Baptist Convention:

We don't have to get together.

The Southern Baptist Convention
doesn't have to survive.

I don't have to be the pastor of Bellevue.

I don't have to live!

But I'm not going to compromise the Word of God.

Everything that's not nailed down with a nail of grace and the hammer of God's Word is going to be *shaken* out of place by His judgment.

These hath God married
    and no man shall part:
        dust on the Bible
           and drought in the heart.

Having truth decay?
Brush up on your Bible!

If God didn't mean what He said,

  why didn't He say what He meant?

Much of **God's will** for your life
is already found in the Bible.

*P*rophecy is history *pre-written*.

Scriptural hope is NOT wishful thinking.
It's rock-solid assurance!

*H*ow to understand a Bible passage:

Read it through.

Think it clear.

Write it down.

Pray it in.

Live it out.

Pass it on.

There are **three kinds** of people in this world: those who are afraid, those who don't know enough to be afraid, and those who know their Bible.

The Bible is a supernatural, spiritual, sovereign, surviving, sustaining, supercharged book about my Savior.

The Bible is God's road map.

The Bible is
God's *love letter*
to His people.

The Bible says all these things happened to them for examples to us. The Bible is more than history; it is devotional literature.

The more of the WORD OF GOD you give away, the more of it will stick to you.

When you look at the Bible and try to understand the Bible, you have to ask three questions:

- What did it mean then?
- How does it apply now?
- How does it apply to me personally?

You haven't gotten into the Bible until you ask that third question.

Anytime you see a therefore in the Bible,
STOP
and see what it's there for.

Want more faith? Get into God's Word.

We need to stop treating the Bible like a math book
and start reading it as a love story.

If you can get past Genesis 1:1, you'll never have trouble with any of the miracles.

If you pray Scripture,
you can be sure you are praying the will of God.

On why he preached the Word of God:
I'M NOT SMART ENOUGH
to preach anything else,
AND I'M TOO SMART
to preach anything else.

There are
two messages
in the Bible:

Come & Go

How can we know
the God of the Bible
if we don't know
the Bible of God?

There are over 7,000
promises in His Word,
and He keeps them all!

THE *W*ORD OF *G*OD

A parable

is an earthly story
with a heavenly meaning.

*E*very now and then

science may disagree with the Bible.

Just give the scientists time,

and maybe they will catch up.

Every one of us will be known for something

when we are gone.

Do you know what I want them to think of

when they think about me?

The Gospel of Christ.

I want them to say, "That man's life was

centered in the only message that

really matters."

The Word of God is more sure
than anything
we see, hear,
feel, or think.

The Bible is a window in this prison world
through which we may look into eternity.

This Word
is the passion of God
for the world,
not tit-for-tat theology.

Study the Bible
to know about God.
Obey the Bible
to really know God.

Tell it to them like it is in the Bible,
and if they want to argue about it
tell them to argue with God.

Cut the Bible anywhere,
and it will bleed.

The blood of Jesus
stains every page.

Point people to
Scripture
and then
get out of the way.

*R*ead the Bible.
It'll give you a check up
from the neck up,
help you avoid stinkin' thinkin',
and totally eliminate
hardening of the attitude.

$\mathcal{W}$ithout the Word of God,
we only have a holy hunch,
and that simply will not do!

As Christians
we are to be newsboys
and not editors of the Gospel.

Many times,
a man has preached a funeral for the Bible,
but the corpse has outlived the pallbearers.

*P*RAYER

*S*atan can't keep God
from answering
our prayers,
but he will keep us
from asking.

The prayer
that gets to heaven
is the *prayer*
that starts in heaven.

God should be our first thought,
not our last resort.

Pray and doubt;
    you'll do without.
        Pray and believe;
            you will receive.

Sometimes we don't feel like praying. But if there were ever a time that we need to pray, it's when we don't feel like it. We need to pray until we do feel like it.

We should pray as if it all depends on God
and then work as if it all depends on us.

What God says to me
is more important
than *what I say to Him.*

Your spiritual life
will never rise above your prayer life.

When trials come, don't wring
your hands—bend your knees.

A lot of **kneeling** will keep you in good **standing**.

Courage is **fear** that has said its **prayers**.

*D*on't give God instructions; just **report for duty!**

There are too many spiritual forgers signing
Jesus' name to their prayer checks.

The greatest problem we face
is not *unanswered* prayer
but *unoffered* prayer.

There is
no sin in your life
that proper prayer could not avoid
or no need
that proper prayer could not supply.

Tragically, many of our prayers
    are so *vague*
        that if God were to answer them,
           we wouldn't even *know* it.

❧

*G*od's delays aren't God's denials.

❧

You can't use a prayer as a smokescreen to keep
you from repentance.

*P*rayer is the greatest Christian privilege.

❧

We can do more than pray after we've prayed, but we can do no more than pray until we've prayed.

❧

Prayer is the *Holy Spirit* finding a desire in the heart of the Father, putting that desire in our hearts to return it in the form of a request to Him.

We need to pull some of the groans out of
our prayers and shove in more
HALLELUJAHs.

—Billy Sunday

Getting into the *Bible* prompts us to pray.

God always answers prayer in a way
that will give Himself glory.

*P*RAYER

If you have the right to **want** something,
you have the right to **pray** for it.

Prayer is never an excuse for LAZINESS.

Prayer is *not* talking God into doing
something that He ordinarily
would not want to do.

*P*rayer will make man cease from sin.
Sin will make man cease from prayer.

—John Bunyan

If it's big enough
to concern you,
it's big enough
to concern God.

FAITH is the medium of exchange in heaven.
If you need an answer to prayer,
spend a little faith.

It's not the length
of the prayer
but the depth
that counts.

God gave you
His unlisted telephone number
and invites you to
get in touch with Him
anytime.

Anything that distracts from vital prayer
in our lives is a treacherous thing. It steals
from us the blessings the Father longs to bestow,
and it takes from the Father the
glory He so richly deserves.

Praise infuses
the energy of God
and confuses
the enemies of God.

PRAY:
"Lord, make me willing
to be made willing."

When
there
is not hope
on the horizontal level,
there's always
hope
on the
vertical
level.

Prayerlessness
is a spirit of
independence from God.

When we pray for rain,
we ought to carry
an umbrella.

You deny yourself when you don't pray.
Prayer is the key
that
unlocks *heaven's treasury.*

Prayer is not getting ready to serve.
Prayer is service.

THE *F*RUIT OF THE *S*PIRIT

*G*od prefers
fruits of the Spirit
over spiritual nuts.

Happiness depends on what happens.
Joy depends on the Lord.

✤

Happiness is like a thermometer—
it registers conditions.
Joy is like a thermostat—
it controls them.

✤

He who angers you, controls you!

Humility is knowing what I am,
acknowledging that God made me that way,
and giving Him glory for it.

Joy is important in winning people to Christ.
Don't go around looking like an advance
agent for the undertaker.

Meekness is
STRENGTH UNDER CONTROL.

Peace is not the subtraction of problems.
It is the addition of power
　　　　to meet those problems.

The joy of the Lord isn't there to remove
the pain; the joy of the Lord is there to
help me bear it.

A "joyless Christian" is an oxymoron.

Joy is proof that what we have is real
and that it satisfies.

Justice is God giving us what we deserve.
Mercy is God not giving us what we deserve.
And grace is God giving us
what we don't deserve.

Mercy is *sympathy* with legs.

Nothing sets a man out of the devil's reach
so much as *humility*.

—Jonathan Edwards

Patience doesn't grimly wait for the end.
It radiantly waits for the dawn.

We should want to be

surprised by joy

and not anticipate trouble.

*S*erenity is not freedom from the storm

but peace amid the storm.

GROWING IN GRACE

If we believe
what we believe,
why do we do
what we do?

God's plan is to
take ordinary people with ordinary talents,
do extraordinary things through them,
and give glory to Himself.

God loves us just the way we are.
But He loves us too much
to leave us that way.

Holiness is not the way to Christ.
Christ is the way to holiness.

If it'll make you healthy, happy, holy, or wholesome—
God says, *"Help yourself!"*

*G*od doesn't want me
to do anything for Him.
He wants to do
something through me.

If the Christian life is lived out in my house,
it will be lived by Jesus.
He is the *only One* Who ever has or
ever will live the Christian life.

Why should God give you
more light when you've
not lived up to the
light you have?

The most miserable man on Earth is not an unsaved
man. The most miserable man on Earth is
a saved man out of fellowship
with Jesus Christ.

Don't ever insult God by saying that He
cannot use you.

The best way to know God's will for the rest of your
life is to DO His will right now.

It's hard to steer a ship that's not moving.

God does not *change* us in order to love us.

He *loves* us in order to change us.

Discipline says, "I need to."
Duty says, "I ought to."
Devotion says, "I want to."

I don't find the will of God.

The will of God finds *me*,

and I respond to it.

Reformation without transformation
leads to greater degradation.

God's will for you is not a roadmap;
it is a relationship.

When I got saved, I gave all that I knew of me to all I knew of Jesus. Since then, I have learned a whole lot more about me and a whole lot more about Jesus. And I've done more repenting and trusting AFTER I got saved than I did WHEN I got saved.

I'm no better than my *devotional life*.

If you are not *growing* in grace,
you are living in disgrace.

*I*s what I'm living for
worth Christ dying for?

The Great Commission is not an option to be considered but a command to be obeyed.

—Hudson Taylor

The task ahead of us
is never as great
as the Power behind us.

The definition of failure
is succeeding at the wrong thing.

God has a purpose and plan for me
that *no one else* can fulfill.

❧

Stress is the gap between
the demands placed on us
and our ability to meet those demands.

❧

What you think and do should agree
with what you say.

WHERE GOD GUIDES, GOD PROVIDES.
Whom God chooses, He uses.

When you get saved,
every place is a holy place
and *every* day is a holy day.

People say, "Get right with Jesus; you may die."
I say, "Get right with Jesus; you may live!"

Exercise daily. Walk with the Lord!

A Christian
who doesn't witness is a
contradiction in terms.

'Tis one life; will soon be past.
Only what's
done for Christ will last.

The freedom that Jesus gives
is not freedom to do what we want,
but the freedom to do as you ought.

Don't be so worried about getting out of trouble
as about getting into righteousness.

A Christian is not a pessimist.
Nor is he a dewy-eyed optimist.
He is a realist
who must visualize
and see the situation as it is.

God blesses you
to make you a blessing.

It is more important
to influence people
than to impress them.

Grace
is the desire
and ability
to do the will of God.

If you get your theology
from circumstances,
you will come to the conclusion
that God does not love you.

There is no cheap, easy, or lazy
way to serve God.

If there were ever a time
you loved Jesus more
than you do at this moment,
you're backslidden.

God's work,
done in God's way,
will never ever want for
God's provision or God's protection.

In all spiritual things
we should be natural.
And in all natural things
we should be spiritual.

On our list of activities in life:
There are
some things we need to eliminate,
some things we need to delegate,
and the rest we need to dedicate.

It's *my* business to do God's business,
and it's *His* business to take care of my business.

It's the set of the *soul*
　　　that determines the goal
　　　　　　and not the *problems* or strife.

Jesus Christ is the LIGHT.
There is no reason for you to stumble
in darkness
when you can walk in the Light.

The Bible does not say,
"Don't walk in the flesh and you will
fulfill the desires of the Spirit."
Rather, it says,
"Walk in the Spirit and you
won't fulfill the desires of the flesh."

Many folks
are plowing water and shoveling smoke.

They're
living to exist and existing to live,

but they
do not have a PURPOSE for life.

My wedding ring doesn't make me *married*,
but it shows I am.

Being baptized doesn't make me a *Christian*
any more than my ring makes
me married.

Baptism, whether a spoonful or a tankful,
will never save anyone.

Sometimes
the most spiritual thing we can do
is *rest*.

The progression of faith:

God accepts me;
that's grace.

Then I accept God's acceptance of me;
that's faith.

Then I accept myself;
that's peace.

Then I can accept you;
that's love.

Then you are free to accept me;
that's fellowship.

The best argument *for*
Christianity and the
best argument *against*
Christianity is the life of
a Christian. Not only are
we to be His witnesses;
we ought to be part of
the evidence.

The Christian life is like riding a bicycle;
you are either *moving ahead*
or falling off.

We'll *find God*
right where
we *left* Him.

The Holy Spirit is not for your enjoyment
but for employment.

To believe in heaven
is not to run away from life;
it is to run toward it.

$\mathcal{I}$ walked a mile with pleasure.

She chatted all the way.

But left me none the wiser for all she had to say.

I walked a mile with sorrow

and not a word said she.

But oh the things I learned from sorrow

when sorrow walked with me.

—William Barclay

When you take a stand
for truth,
you're going to have a head-on collision
with error.

*I*f we just prune the limbs
(of bad habits),
we just
strengthen the roots.

We *pray* without crying,
give without sacrificing,
and *live* without fasting.

Is it any wonder that
we *sow* without reaping?

We should never fear the will of God.

We ought to be *living*
as if Jesus *died* yesterday,
rose this morning,
and is *coming back* this
afternoon.

Where there is no faith for the future,
there is no work for the present.

With *grace* there is nothing to earn,
but much to *learn*.

I tell people to **KEEP THE FAITH**.
And that's true.
But we should also give it away.
If you have no desire to give it *away*,
perhaps you ought to give it *up*.

You don't **need** more
until you **claim** what you already have.

You can't say,

"Lord, show me Your will for my life and then

I'll make up my mind whether I want to do it."

You just simply hand God a blank sheet of

paper, sign your name at the bottom, and say,

"Lord, You fill in the details."

❧

Your character
is the
harvest of *your habits.*

Victorious Living

Faith is
belief
with legs on it.

Everything we truly believe, we obey.

Everything else is just religious talk.

Faith is the response of the heart

to the *character* of God.

*F*aith that can't be tested can't be trusted.

It's the object of your faith that matters,
not the strength of it.

Obedience
is the greatest proof of devotion.

Sin cannot win. Faith cannot fail.

Plan ahead.
It wasn't raining when Noah built the ark.

Faith is not so much receiving from God what
we want but accepting from God what
He gives.

Sorrow looks back;

worry looks around;

but faith looks up.

The reason that God honors *faith*

is that *faith* honors God.

Do you want to live
a supernatural life of *victory?*
The Victory Express
runs on two tracks: *trust* and *obey*.

Faith believes in spite of the circumstances and acts
in spite of the consequences.

Faith is like a roll of film:
it develops best in the dark.

❧

Faith is not *believing* that God can do something.
Faith is *knowing* that He will.

❧

Praise is faith turned inside out.

Faith says *please*. Praise says *thank you*.

Fear knocked.

Faith answered.

No one was there.

Don't put your FAITH in faith.
That would be like looking *at* the telescope
and not *through* it.

$\mathcal{D}$on't thank Him by feeling.
Thank Him by faith.

Faith is believing in God
in spite of appearances.

$\mathcal{F}aith$ is God's cure for fretting.

$\mathcal{D}elight$ is God's cure for depression.

$\mathcal{C}ommitment$ is God's cure for concern.

$\mathcal{R}est$ is God's cure for resentment.

VICTORY is not achieved by fighting.
It is achieved by faith.

Christ won't transform my problem until I
transfer it to Him.

Don't put a question mark where God
has put a period.

Faith is divine in conception,
        unique in character, and
                complete in unity.

❧

Grace says,
"I love you,"
reaching down.

Faith says,
"I believe you,"
reaching up.

*F*aith possesses what grace provides.

*G*od's omnipotence
 plus our obedience
  equals miracle living.

We do not fight for victory;
we fight from victory.
The victory was won at Calvary!

Man is SAVED by faith alone,
but the faith that saves
is never alone.

*G*od's will is not something you *have* to do;
it's something you *get* to do.

True Worship:

All that I am

responding to all that He is

in gratitude and praise.

$\mathcal{A}$ Christian
with a glowing witness
is worth a library
full of arguments.

If there is no opposition, there is no victory.

Exalt the Savior,

edify the saint,

and evangelize the sinner;

that's what we're here for.

Faith is taking God at His Word.

Faith

sees the invisible,

believes the incredible,

knows the unknowable,

and receives the impossible.

God doesn't want you to serve Him in *your*
poor little old weak way. He wants you to serve
Him in *His* mighty, dynamic way.

ADRIANISMS

God is not interested so much in making you happy and healthy as He is in making you holy.

It is only the life that is lived with the approval of Jesus and in the authority of Jesus that will bring acclaim to Jesus.

We become like what we worship.
True worship will make us more like God.

If you are saved,
you will have a desire to be holy, a hunger for
the Word, the inner witness of the Spirit,
and a desire to share Jesus.
These are the birthmarks of the believer.

On the Christian's lack of power:
You've been to Calvary for pardon,
but you haven't been to Pentecost for power.

Thanksgiving enjoys the gift.
Praise enjoys the Giver.

There are three heavens.

The first heaven is where the birds fly;
the second heaven is where the stars are;
and the third heaven is the abode of God.

The first heaven we see by day;
the second heaven we see by night;
and the third heaven we see by faith.

THE LORD never said,
"I'll show you…then you'll believe."
He said, "Believe.
Then I'll show you."

The *least* amount of faith
is greater than
the *greatest* amount of difficulty.

A Christian with a testimony
is never at the mercy of
an unbeliever with an argument.

We are all to bring all men
by all means to Jesus
at any cost.

Worship is doing everything in the
name of Jesus and giving God thanks for it.

When the

child of God

loves the Word of God

and *sees* the Son of God,

He is changed

by the Spirit of God

into the image of God

for the glory of God

because he has found

the *truth* of God.

Worship is enjoying the presence of *God*.

To those who believe,

nothing is impossible.

To those who do *not* believe,

nothing is possible.

We are called to be witnesses
not lawyers.

You must be *seeking*

the face of God

in order for Him to guide you

by His eye.

Obedience is

a duty to be performed,

a debt to be paid,

a delight to be preferred,

and

a decision to be practiced.

A WORD TO THE WISE

A proverb is a
general principle,
generally applied
that brings a
general result.

Character is what we are in the dark.

God did not call us to
sit, soak, and sour,
but to
serve.

You have all of God you want.
If you don't have any more, it's because
you're satisfied
like you are.

It's not the pastor's job to fill the pew.
It's his job to fill the pulpit.

LUKEWARM Christians
are the alibi of sinners.

Teach men their *rights*,
    and you have a revolution.

Teach them their *responsibilities*,
    and you have a revival.

*A*nything God orders
He will pay the bill for.

*D*ecision determines destiny.

God does business
with those who mean business.

God doesn't *appreciate* what
He doesn't *initiate*.

If you are not in a storm right now, I am happy
for you. Enjoy it! But just wait a while.
Sooner or later, you will be.

There's enough time in every day
to do gracefully
everything God wants you to do.

Time is what God allows so everything doesn't happen to us **all at once**.

❧

You can save a lot of time by waiting on God.

❧

A *faith*
that *fizzles*
before the *finish*
had a *flaw*
from the *first*.

When you are not afraid of dying,
only then can you live.

Every child of God
is a chip off the old Block.

Good things
become bad things
when they keep you
from the best things.

If you try to turn *proverbs into promises*,
you'll lose your religion.

Life is lived in depth—not length.

Nothing is politically right that is morally wrong.

*Y*our reputation is your actions.
Your character is your reactions.

The grace of God will *exalt* a person
without inflating him
and will *humble* a person
without debasing him.

*W*e set the sail; God makes the wind.

We're not in a race.
We're in a pilgrimage.

*C*ut yourself loose from yesterday.

PREACHING
is not filling a bucket; it's lighting a torch.

Reputation is what others think about you;
character is what God knows about you.

There is no panic in heaven, only plans.

—Corrie Ten Boom

Whatever man does without God,
he will fail miserably
or succeed even more miserably.

When God develops inner character,
He is never in a hurry.

You will be wise to let God
keep the books.

Work is no substitute for worship.

A proverb is a
short sentence
based on
long experience.

—Miguel de Cervantes

A secret
is something we tell
one person at a time.

Advice to children:
"Love God, hate sin, and watch for trucks!"

$\mathcal{B}$eyond the shadow of any doubt
or peradventure…

Squeeze the juice out of each day.

The same sun that melts ice
hardens clay.

Confession
is faith
turned inside out.

If you deny the past,
you'll distort the future.

Everyone has a right to his own opinion,
but *no one* has a right to be wrong
about the facts.

Making one BIG DECISION
will cover a lot of small ones.

If you live as if there is no God,
you'd better be right.

In *finding fault:*
It's a thin pancake that doesn't have two sides.

.

It's what you sow that multiplies,
 not what you keep in the barn.

—Stanley Tam

Leave
the woodpile
higher
than you found it.

If you live for this world,
 you are in the junk business.
 It is all premature junk.

_N_ever pull your radishes up by the roots to
see how they are growing.

On the MYTHS found in New-Ageism:
Man cannot turn into God by being nice
any more than
he can turn into a flower by wearing perfume.

Pain is inevitable,
but
misery is optional.

Silence isn't always golden.

Sometimes, it's just plain yellow.

Some people can't find Christ
for the same reason a thief can't find
a policeman.

Anything that **begins** with "we"
will **end** in nothing.

The stone wasn't rolled away
to let Jesus *out.*
It was rolled away
to let the disciples *in.*

There are no **natural** laws.
They are *God's* laws;
nature obeys them.

The **will** of God won't
take you where the
grace of God
can't keep you.

A *W*ORD TO THE *W*ISE

There are *two classes* of people
in this world:
those who take things for granted
and those who take things with gratitude.

There was a time
when you were not;
there never will be a time
when you will not be.

When I cease to be better,
I cease to be good.

To think that
Washington is going to be the answer
to the world's problems is like
rearranging the deck chairs on the **Titanic**.

Watch your words. Make them *warm* and *sweet*
because you may have to eat them.

To look for **scientific proof** of God
would be like taking a piano apart
to look for a song.

We live in a day where a hero is a sandwich,
Life is a magazine, Power is a candy bar,
Joy is a detergent, Sin is a perfume,
a star is an actress
who's been married three times,
and the "Real Thing" is a soft drink.
We need to wake up!

When a man jumps out of a ten-story building,
he doesn't break the law of gravity;
he demonstrates it.

When you can't tell where a
man stands,
you already know.

When you die, you are going to leave
behind all that you *have*, and you are going to
take with you all that you *are*.

You *always* reap
what you sow.
You reap
later than you sow,
and you reap
more than you sow.

*W*here there is light,
there is bugs.

You cannot legislate morality; you can only legislate
against immorality.

Without a knowledge of Jesus,
all education is but splendid ignorance.
If you educate people without a knowledge
of our Lord, you make them clever devils.

You can tell the size of a Christian
by what it takes to stop him.

You can't sweeten
the well by
painting the pump.

WISDOM is not getting all wet around the lashes
and warm around the heart. It is having
a mind that is stayed on God,
full of the Word of God,
and led by the Spirit of God.

A WORD TO THE WISE

Wisdom
is
uncommon
sense.

We have
too many idols
and **not enough** heroes.

You have a date
with Deity.

Sometimes
we can be so heavenly minded
we are no earthly good.

You take care of your *character*,
and God will take care of your *reputation*.

RELATIONSHIPS

To Joyce:
"If you ever leave me,
I'm going with you."

I asked Joyce,
"Will you love me when I'm old and gray?"
She answered, "Sure I do."

❧

Forgiveness is *not* an emotion;
it's a choice.

❧

Home is the university of life
with parents as the professors,
children as students,
and life as the lab.

*I*f you marry a child of the devil,
you'll get the devil for a daddy-in-law.

On the uniqueness of men and women:

A *woman* is infinitely superior to a man
at being a woman,
and a *man* is infinitely superior to a woman
at being a man.

We can't deal with our ancestors,
but we can deal with our dependents.

The more I learn about *Jesus*,
the more I love my *wife*.

Today, our children are becoming roadkill on the information superhighway.

The way to find the right person is to be the right person.

GETTING MARRIED

is like buying a phonograph record:

You buy it because you
want what's on one side;

you *just take* what comes
on the other side.

If you would measure your love for your Father,
you must measure your love for your brother.

When my children do not love one another,
it's a disgrace to ME.

If you need encouragement, give it.
If you need love, give it.
Whatever you need, give it away.

On families:
Anything without a head is dead,
and anything with two heads is a freak.

To dwell there *above* with those that we love

will be glory.

To dwell here *below* with those that we know—

well, that's another story.

To be completely known and still be loved

is the goal of marriage.

What some people call burying the hatchet

is just digging up more dirt.

*W*e're to love people and use things
not
love things and use people.

Everyone is talking today
about so-called **"safe sex."**
But sex is not supposed to be dangerous!

When dads shoot straight,
the kids will hit the mark.

I want to remind you girls

that what you are depending on

to catch a man

is what you will have to do

to keep him.

If he loves you because of your beauty,

what are you going to do

when your beauty is no longer there?

On raising children:

Be fair.

Be firm.

Be fun.

If you can be a Christian at home, you can be a Christian anywhere.

On divorce:
Sometimes the marriage that starts out as an *ideal* becomes an *ordeal*, and then they are looking for a *new deal*.

You can't be **right** with God and be **wrong** with a brother.

God made us

different

that He might

make us

one.

A woman is to a man what a wind is to a fire; she can fan it up or blow it out.

I got all "twitopated" when I first met
Joyce Gentry.

It will do you little good to come to church and act
pious around the **Lord's Table**
if you've been bickering around the **breakfast table**.

Love is blind,
but marriage is an eye opener.

Our Lord wants us to
have **three homes:**
a family home,
a church home,
and a heavenly home.

Parents' responsibility:
To create an atmosphere in my home
where my children can with ease
choose to follow God.

Some parents say that their
kids are angels.

You'll find that as their legs grow longer,
their wings
get shorter.

We must take our families back.

Otherwise, the world will
become our children's parent.

When I get home from a trip,

I don't hug the sofa and kiss the lamp.
It's Joyce I want to see.

She's what makes it home for me.
And Jesus is what makes it heaven

not gold streets with jewels—but Jesus.

$\mathcal{T}$here are those who say that children make a rich man poor. No, they have it backward. Children make a poor man rich. A rich man can't take his riches to heaven, but I'm taking my children.

$\mathcal{M}$arriage

is divine in establishment,

supreme in relationship, and

unconditional in commitment.

$\mathscr{E}$NCOURAGEMENT

$\mathscr{I}$t'll lick
the red
off your candy.

All of us fail.
Use your failures as a guidepost
to lead you on.

Be humbly grateful, not grumbly hateful.

God is not here
to keep you out of trouble;
He's here to get in trouble with you.

God is the *Healer* of broken dreams and the *Restorer* of stolen years.

The door to the room of opportunity

swings on the hinges of opposition.

The suffering that you have now
is just the black velvet upon which
the diamond of God's glory
is going to be revealed.

—Charles H. Spurgeon

Do your best and then sleep in peace.
God is awake.

❦

When you are in a storm,
what seems to be a problem to you
is not a problem to God.

Where we cannot trace God's *hand,*
we can trust His *heart.*

Don't judge God
by your circumstances.
If you do, you will
lose your faith.

Failure is *NOT* final.

*G*od's promises are not **mottos** to hang on the wall. They are **checks** to take to the bank.

It is safer *on the waves* with Jesus
than *in the boat* without Him.

It's always too soon to quit
but never too late to start!

When trouble comes to you
and doesn't lead you to *worship God*,
you sure have wasted a lot of trouble.

DOUBT is to my spirit
what pain is to my body.

If you woke up this morning,
and you're still here—
God still has a plan for your life!

Glance at your problems
and *gaze* at your Lord.

Never doubt in the dark
what God has shown you in the light.

God doesn't want to give you

the wings of a dove

to fly away;

He wants to give you

the wings of an eagle

to soar over your problems

right where you are.

*W*e're too blessed to be stressed.

$\mathcal{G}$od promises a safe landing,

not a calm passage.

❧

$\mathcal{J}$ust because something does not make sense
to you does not mean it doesn't make sense.

❧

No matter what is happening in your life,
know that God is waiting for you
with open arms.

What we cannot understand,
we can endure with God.

While the Bible admits
the possibility of failure,
it never assumes
the necessity of it.

When we were *born again*,
we were
born to win.

ENCOURAGEMENT

Attitude,
more than aptitude,
determines
altitude.

Don't whine! *Shine* for Jesus.

Failure in the past
does not nullify
purpose in the future.

$\mathcal{D}$on't be under a burden by other people's criticism. You can't make yourself sick trying to make someone else well.

Jesus takes *nobodies* and turns them into *nobilities*.

God does not flunk any of His children.
He just re-enrolls them.

God will put on us
more than we can bear,
but not more than
He can bear.

If the outlook
looks glum, I want to tell you
the uplook is very bright!

He who has a **why** to live
can bear almost any **how**.

God's going to turn every
tear into a pearl and
string them for a
diadem
for you.

It's not right for the upright
to be uptight.

One of these days,
God is going to pull back the shades of night,
pin them with a star,
open the door of the morning,
and flood your world
with the sunshine
of His love and light.

Let go of this world and take hold of God
with both hands.

Life is meant to be lived on the path,
not in the past.

*J*ust because you
cannot see God
working,
does not mean He is
not at work.

On Satan's attempt to bring us harm:
God uses the ax the devil sharpens.

Satan binds us to the past
while Jesus frees us for the future.

We should live
on the sunny side of *Hallelujah* Avenue where
Glory Road intersects.

Spiritual success is what we become in the
light of what God designed us to be.

The groans we endure are temporary.
The glory we expect is eternal.

Sorrow is a clean wound. Guilt is a dirty wound.
Time and the *grace of God* will heal sorrow.

Trouble can become a seminary to teach us
the provisions of God.

We are responsible for the *effort*,
not the *outcome*.

*T*hat which has been
decreed by heaven
cannot be
annulled by hell.

We don't live by explanations.
We live by promises.

What Jesus says is more certain than
anything we can feel.

What you are is God's gift to you.
What you become is your gift to God.

When God allows darkness
to overshadow your life,
don't light your own fire.

$\mathcal{Y}$ou can't live life in a rearview mirror.

$\mathcal{Y}$ou don't have to know "why."

"Why" is God's question.

"How" is your answer.

When you know that
your future is secure,
you can concentrate on your present.

Why settle for anything less
than God's best for you?

When God says "no,"
it's because He has
something better in
store for you.

Yesterday and tomorrow
need to be taken out of my
calendar of concern.

$\mathcal{S}$IN AND $\mathcal{T}$EMPTATION

$\mathcal{N}$o one has ever
sinned themselves
beyond the
love of God.

Anything you love more, fear more, serve more, or value more than God is your idol.

As Christians we must be in collision with the devil not in collusion with him.

Everything that is not nailed down is coming loose. And the devil is pulling nails as fast as he can.

Bitterness is like an acid that destroys its own container.

Focusing on *feelings*
leads to a *faltering* faith.

$\mathcal{M}$an isn't a sinner
because he sins;
he sins because he is a sinner.

God will test us, but God will not tempt us.

God tests us to make us stand.
Satan tempts us to make us fall.

You cannot **confess to God**
what you will not **admit to yourself.**

۔ِؤ

I'm not always what I think I am,
but I am what I think.

۔ِؤ

If the **devil** never bothers you, it's because
you're both going in the **same direction.**

If the greatest commandment
is to love God with all of your heart,
the greatest sin
is not to do it.

The world is the external foe.
The flesh is the internal foe.
The devil is the infernal foe.

Not only can negative emotions take life from your years, they can take years from your life.

Nothing is more destructive than sin. Sin *fascinates*, and then it *assassinates*. Sin *thrills*, and then it *kills*.

The devil is a knucklehead.

If Satan can't make you bad,
he'll make you busy.

Sin that used to
slink down the back alley
now struts down Main Street.

You can eat the devil's corn if you want to, but he'll choke you on the cob.

—R.G. Lee

SIN will take you
farther than you want to go,
keep you longer than you want to stay,
and cost you more than you want to pay.

On sin:
you'll get what you want,
but you won't want what you get.

The sin of immorality is not one we are instructed to fight. It is one we have been told to flee. Run from that compromising situation. Saturate that place with your absence.

To err is human. To try *to conceal* it is too.

To get to hell, we must climb over
    every prayer,
        every sermon,
            the Word of God,
                and the love of God
                    shown on Calvary.

Whatever Satan can get you to laugh at, you'll never take seriously again.

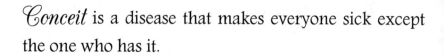

Conceit is a disease that makes everyone sick except the one who has it.

CONSCIENCE
is that thing that
feels bad when everything else
feels good.

Fear is a dark room
where negatives are developed.

$\mathcal{A}$n unguarded strength
is a double weakness.

$\mathcal{G}$ive Satan an inch, and he'll be a ruler.

An excuse is just the skin of a reason
stuffed with a lie.

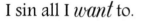

I sin all I *want* to.

I just *don't want* to.

If you are living in IMMORALITY, you're either headed for the woodshed or headed for hell.

It is not enough to confess sin without forsaking it.

*O*n the consequences of sin:
Every kick has a kickback.

Worry is an insult to God.

A thorn in the flesh is nothing
compared to a thorn in the
conscience.

$\mathcal{D}$on't let a little sin in;
all hell will break loose.

$\mathcal{F}lattery$
is a lot like perfume:
sniff it but don't swallow it.

If a person is concerned about committing
the unpardonable sin,
he hasn't committed it.

$\mathcal{D}$efinition of drugs:
instant heaven that leads to everlasting hell.

God has wonderfully made you
where you can't think
two thoughts at one time.
If you're thinking what you ought to be thinking,
you won't be thinking
what you ought not to be thinking.

Gambling is one person's profit and pleasure at
another's pain and loss.

Hypocrites and flatterers are first cousins.

The hypocrite will say behind your back
what he will not say to your face.
The flatterer will say to your face
what he won't say behind your back.

God deals with the devil's crowd on credit
and with Christians on a cash basis.

If Jesus didn't save me from *me*, He didn't
save me from my *worst enemy*.

I have been saved from
the penalty of sin.
I am being saved
from the power of sin.
I will be saved
from the possibility of sin.

Better to die with conviction
than to live with compromise.

$\mathcal{M}$any things are opened by mistake
and none more frequently than the mouth.

🙖

$\mathcal{I}$t's never right to do
wrong, and it's never
wrong to do right.

🙖

It's not the amount of sin,
it's the fact of sin that damns us.
More people are killed in nine feet of water
than in ninety feet.

I've never found anywhere in the Bible

that says smoking would send you to hell,

but it does make you

smell like you've been there.

If you were *sinking* in quicksand,
the devil would pat you on the *head*.

Most of the people in America are egomaniacs who
are strutting their way to hell thinking they're too
good to be damned.

Never give the devil a ride!
He will always want to drive!

On overcoming **temptation:**

If you want to take a bone from a dog,
give him a steak,
and he'll drop the bone.

No man who is morally wrong has the
ability to govern.

On consequences of sin:

There are a lot of folks who think they can sow their wild oats six days a week and then pray for crop failure on Sunday.

Never mistake the man for the moment. No one is perfect.

On political correctness:

The only sin today is to call sin, sin.

Our
sins
were
the nails that nailed Him
to that tree, and our hard
hearts
were
the
hammers
that
drove
those
nails.

Satan is a decided fact,
           a destructive force,
                and a defeated foe.

Rivers and men both
become crooked by
following the path of
least resistance.

Satan is brilliantly stupid
           and hideously beautiful.

Sin and Temptation

SIN is an inside job.

Satan wants to turn
the Ten Commandments
into
the Ten Suggestions
since a law without
penalty is merely advice.

Some people are so *arrogant*
they can strut sitting down.

Satan rules a doomed domain
and sails a sinking ship
Why follow a loser?

Sin is not just breaking God's laws;
it is breaking His heart.

Satan wants to
CRIPPLE me
and then
blame me for limping.

Sin and Temptation

Some people try to

drown

their problems.

Don't they know that problems can

swim?

Talking to teenagers about *premarital sex:*

If you eat your cake now,
you'll have a crummy tomorrow.

Sow a thought—reap a deed.
Sow a deed—reap a character.
Sow a character—reap a destiny.

Sometimes the *ravages* of sin preempt the *blessings* of God.

TEMPTATION is trying
to get us to fulfill a
legitimate desire in an
illegitimate way.

The devil would rather start a church fuss
than sell a barrel of whiskey.

The devil's too smart
to go fishing without any bait.

There has never been an argument,
a war,
a divorce,
or a church split
that was not caused by pride.

The greatest sin for a Christian is
silence.

The heart of the human problem is the
problem of the human heart.

The opposite of truth is *not* error;
the opposite of truth is
SIN.

The fraying of America's social fabric is fast
becoming a national obsession.

Unbelief is the supreme evil
and the source of all other sin.

✤

*W*e don't need isolation from evil;
we need insulation from it.

✤

We are sinners because of
who we are, not what we do.

We do not lose our salvation when we sin.
But if we persist,
we indeed will lose the joy of our salvation.

We *amuse* ourselves
with the things that *break* Christ's heart.

We don't do anything perfectly,
but sin.

Worry is pulling tomorrow's clouds over today's sunshine.

When you're saved,
God doesn't fix you to
where you can't sin
anymore
but where you can't sin
and enjoy it.

Where my mind is,
my feet will follow.

Why should God give you more strength to
serve the devil?

Your enemy is not the Republicans,

the Democrats,

or the Internal Revenue Service.

Your enemy is not your wife

or your wife's family.

It's not the pornographer, the liquor baron,

or the drug pusher.

These are all flesh and blood.

We have a common enemy with them—

his name is *Satan.*

Worry looks at God through the circumstances.
Peace looks at circumstances through God.

You say,
"I'm not afraid of the devil."
That's not enough.
He ought to be afraid of you.

PRIDE is #1 on God's hate parade.

Worry is an admission
that I'm putting something before God.

When a person gets sick in the stomach from
drinking,
his stomach has *more sense* than his head.

Proud men at their best are
sinners at their worst.

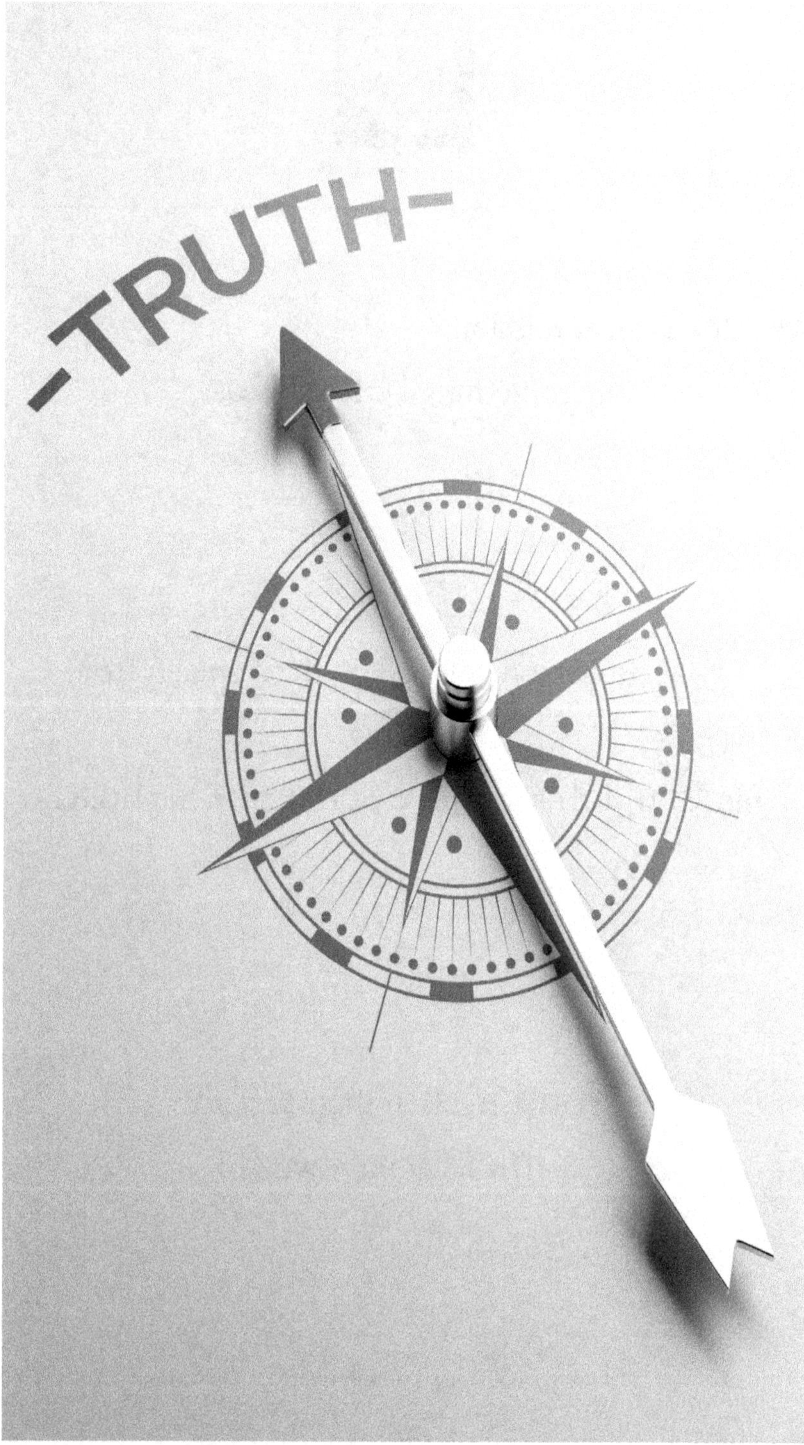
-TRUTH-

*T*RUTH

*W*e don't have to agree.
You have the right
to be wrong
if you want to.

It's better to be **divided** by truth
than **united** in error.

Wisdom has two parts:

1. Having a lot to say.

2. Not saying it.

Don't let your conscience
be your guide
unless God guides your conscience.

I know some of you don't like what I've said. If I've made any of you **angry**, just come up to me after the sermon and apologize. I'll **forgive** you.

Nothing *ruins* the truth
like stretching it.

It's better to be *hated*
for telling the **truth** than
loved for telling a **lie**.

Knowledge comes from looking **around;**
wisdom comes from looking **up.**

The truest thing about me is
what God says about me.

When you're right,
you can afford to keep your temper.
When you're wrong,
you can't afford to lose it!

Wisdom
is seeing life
from God's point of view.

*W*isdom is the gumption
to function
with unction.

Wisdom is the power to see and the inclination to choose the best and highest goals with the surest means of obtaining them.

Atheists really mean they don't want God rather than they believe there is no God.

Facts are like a recipe. Truth is like the meal.
You don't eat the cookbook; you eat the meal.
Digest a truth, and it will change your life.

Evolution is *not* science;
it's science fiction.

If you please God,
    it doesn't matter whom you displease.
If you displease God,
    it doesn't matter whom you please.

Truth

It's better to know the truth and to stand alone than it is to be wrong with a multitude.

It's better to
speak truth
that hurts and then helps
than falsehood
that comforts and then kills.

It's better to ultimately succeed
with the truth
than to temporarily succeed
with a lie.

Loveless truth is brutal.
Truthless love is hypocrisy.
Love in truth is necessary.

On defeating concepts such as atheism and liberalism:

You cannot kill an idea with a bullet. The only thing that will shoot down an idea is
a better idea.

We need to be very cautious about being spokespersons for God.

𝒯RUTH

CHAPTER
THIRTEEN

The Church

Too often,
our churches are
sacred societies
for the
snubbing of sinners.

On attending a large church:

*J*ust sit somewhere in the first ten rows and
don't look back.

Some people go to church
three times in their lives:
when they're born,
when they're married,
and when they die—
hatched, matched, and dispatched.
The first time they throw water,
the second time rice,
and the third time dirt.

Going to church doesn't make you a Christian any more than going in the garage will make you an automobile.

—Billy Sunday

If your religion hasn't *changed your life*, you had better *change your religion*.

In the OLD TESTAMENT,
God had a *temple for His people*.
In the NEW TESTAMENT,
God has a *people for His temple*.

THE Church

267

On church unity:
We are to be brothers
without being *twins*.

Our churches ought to run on the engine of prayer.

Religion without
repentance is
repugnant to God.

The biggest cult
is the cult of the comfortable.

The Mission of the Church: *make* them,
mark them, and
mature them.

Your absence from church
is a vote to close its doors.

—R.G. Lee (paraphrased)

THE CHURCH

I'm weary of hearing about the religious right and the religious left.
The issue is not right or left;
the issue is right or wrong.

I'm firmly convinced that if we would
clean up the pulpits of America,
we'd go a long way to cleaning up America.

The devil would just as soon send you to hell
from the pew as he had the gutter.

Get everybody to *love Jesus*, and you've got a wonderful church. They don't have to agree on anything else.

False religion
is characterized by force.

True religion
is characterized by faith.

GROWING churches love,
and loving churches grow.

Most religion in America is man–centered religion rather than God-centered. People are looking for religion to serve them.

The Church is a society of sinners

who finally admitted it.

This building is *not* the church.

It's just a sheep shed.

We don't come to church to worship.

We bring our worship to church.

A church will either

evangelize

or it will

fossilize,

but it will not stand still.

Some people come to church with a sign

around their neck that says,

"Do not disturb."

THE *C*HURCH

It's easier to cool down a zealot
than it is to warm up a corpse.

On bringing all men by all means:
Every program is a stretcher to bring people in on.

The Church
is *not*
a showboat;
it's a
battleship.

$\mathcal{M}$any of us talk a good religion. We're like the young man who called his girlfriend and said, "Sweetheart, you are so precious to me. I love you so much. I'd fight wild beasts to be by your side. I'd tread on broken glass to hold your hand. And if it doesn't rain, I'm going to come over and see you tomorrow night."

If a church isn't *supernatural,*
it's *superficial.*

The seven last words of churches
today might be,
"We never did it that way before."

❧

Revival begins not in the state house or
the White House, but in the church house
and in your house and my house.

The Church is *not a*
museum for saints;
it's a hospital for sinners.

The Church
is the only organization, except
for Hell's Angels, that a person has to confess
that he's been bad before he can join.

Money

What you do not
freely give,
God neither
needs nor wants.

Bring *God's* tithe
into *God's* house
on *God's* day
that *God's* work
might be done in *God's* way.

To whom little is not enough, nothing is enough.

—Epicurus (paraphrased)

Do your givin' while you're livin',
then you'll be knowin' where it's goin'.

—Ann Landers

Tithing is not God's way to raise money.
It's His way to grow Christians.

When it comes to giving, some people stop
at nothing.

You can give without loving,
but you can't
love without giving.

You'll see how rich you are when you add up everything you have that money can't buy and death can't take away.

Lack of *wealth*
cannot take away
genuine *contentment*.

Don't cling to things so tightly
that it will hurt
when God
has to pry open your fingers to take them.

Give God the chance to provide
before you buy.

If we could take it with us, it would melt where some
of us are going.

—Billy Sunday

Some people have made a god of wealth.
They worship at the shrine of money.
Their god is gold. Their creed is greed.
Their theology is

> "Get all you can; can all you get;
> sit on the lid; and poison the rest."

ℳONEY

The problem many of us have
is not wanting more
but wanting more than somebody else.

***

We try to keep up with the Joneses.
But when we finally catch up with them,
they refinance.

***

We spend the first half of our lives wasting our health to get wealth; the second half of our lives we spend our wealth to get back our health.

How sad to rise in the judgment
and meet a God that *you do not know*
because somehow you put your trust in
riches rather than in Him.

Don't give until it hurts;
give until it feels good.

The things of this world will never satisfy
the longings of your heart.
A round world cannot fit
into a three-cornered heart.

$\mathcal{G}$od is going to meet our **needs**, not our wants. I have needed things that *I didn't want.*

My dad used to say, "You **need** a spanking."

Give God what's **right**,

not what's left!

On tithing:

Abraham commenced it;

Jacob continued it;

Malachi commanded it;

Jesus commended it.

Who are you to cancel it?

*G*od will meet our **need**
not our greed.

Just for Fun

I may be a nut,
but I'm fastened
to a good bolt,
the Lord Jesus Christ.

In my
humble but accurate
opinion…

Do you know where Greece came from?
It oozed out of Turkey.

It's a terrible thing for a man
to think he has the gift of preaching
when nobody has the gift of *listening!*

*On acting **religious**:*

It's like a pig. You can scrub him clean, brush his teeth, and dress him in a pink ribbon, but he will go right back into the mire. A scrubbing on the outside doesn't change his inner nature.

*O*n the demons entering the pigs:
Those pigs committed hog-i-cide.

If you wrestle with a pig, you'll both get dirty;
but the pig will love it.

Birthdays are good for you. The more you have, the longer you live.

Name for young preachers
or seminary students:
EMBRYONIC THEOLOGS

There are some things we can't be dogmatic about. But there are other things we can be bull-dogmatic about.

—Dr. Joseph Conrad

*S*ome say it's a sin for a woman to wear
makeup. I say it's a sin for some women
NOT to wear makeup!

*O*n the Israelites eating manna
in the wilderness:
Manna in the morning,
manna in the evening,
manna at suppertime.

*P*ut it down big, plain, and straight…

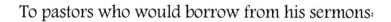

To pastors who would borrow from his sermons:

If what I preach fits your gun, then shoot it.
But use your own powder.

Wisdom doesn't necessarily come with old age.
Sometimes, old age just shows up by itself.

—Tom Wilson

Sound theology will make you feel better.

On gossips:
>> Don't let them use your ears
>> for garbage cans.

The Christian life is not all honey and no bees.

We're not going to slack up,
>> let up,
>> or shut up
>> 'til we're *taken up*.

When someone does you wrong,
tell Jesus on them.

Beauty is skin deep,
but ugly goes all the way to the bone.
Beauty fades,
but ugly holds its own.

I've never seen a bride
that wasn't *beautiful.*
I have seen some
that *just did make it.*

What's down in the well

comes up in the bucket.

Jonah slept on a foam blubber mattress.

Some people *brighten* up a room

just by *leaving*.

*Y*outh looks forward;
old age looks back;
and middle age just looks frustrated.

Alka Seltzer Christians fizzle for a little while and then
disappear.

On problems:
I got 'em;

you got 'em;

Adam had 'em.

Samson had the most *expensive* haircut in history.

*S*ome people sing like a frog
with a man in its throat.

When you were born, you *cried* and people around you
laughed. Make sure when you die, you will *laugh* and
people around you will *cry.*

A man wrote a woman one letter a day
for two years.
She ended up *marrying…*

the mailman.

EPITAPH on tombstone of Mr. Solomon Peas:

This ain't peas; it's just the pod.
Peas shelled out and went to God.

I can carry a tune.
I just can't unload it.

I traced my FAMILY.
We go all the way back
to a crooked farmer
and a drunken sailor—
the farmer was Adam
and the sailor was
Noah.

Don't make decisions by majority vote.
The majority is almost always wrong.

Five out of every four people
have trouble with FRACTIONS.

Said one demon to another:
If Christ ever gets out of that tomb,
hell help us, all heaven will break loose.

Instead of a culture of common
good,
we have culture of constant
complaint.

If we are what we think,
it's a wonder I didn't turn into a girl back in high school.

There are too many Christians out in the back alley eating tin cans with the devil's billy goats.

I'm what they call a prison singer: always behind a few bars and looking for the right key.

When asked whether telling the devil
to leave you alone is like praying to him:
You are not praying to a cat
when you say scat.

There are TWO CLASSES of people:
the saints
and the ain'ts.

You have to watch a man that says he understands
women because he'll lie about anything.

When you *lay an egg*...the best thing to do is
stand back and *admire it!*

I can't get *too mad* when

somebody says something bad about me.

I'm just thankful

that he doesn't know *anything else.*

*W*hat I'm full of is what
comes out when I'm
jostled.

Heaven

When my time comes,
don't be sorry for me.
I'll be kicking up gold dust
on the streets of glory!

Death is only a comma to a Christian—
not a period.

Christ is my *inheritance;*
heaven is the safe deposit box.

The devil gives the best first and the worst last,
but the Lord saves the best for last.

We're not going to heaven by the "rocket of reason" or the "ladder of logic," but by the "railroad of redemption"—the old T & O—trust and obey.

Works don't **lead** us to heaven;
they **follow** us to heaven.

Eternity is only a breath away.

If Jesus is still in the grave, your hope of heaven is not worth half a hallelujah.

I'm looking forward to eternity.
I made reservations in the
non-smoking section.

There are only two places where there's no hope. One is in hell because when you go to hell, you've lost hope. The other is in heaven because when you're in heaven, *you don't need hope.*

A rich man is poor
when he has no treasure in heaven.

PREACHERS AND PREACHING

Without stutter, stammer, apology, or equivocation...

A young preacher used to preach
"Thou shalt not."

Then he began to preach
"Thou shalt."

Finally, he began to preach
"Thou."

*B*efore I preach, I kneel before God.
Often I will tell Him out loud
what I am going to preach.
If I can't feel good about that,
I don't preach it.

$\mathcal{P}$reach the whole Bible.
The Bible is not full of holes.

Description of his ministry:

Preaching the Word
as it is
for men
as they are.

I would be a
sheer, unmitigated fool
to stand up here and try to preach
with a heart that is not clean and not pure.

If there is no hell
in the pulpits,
there will be plenty
in the streets.

I have endeavored to
preach Christ.

I'm just the delivery boy.

On false prophets:

*W*hen you look for the devil,

never fail to look in the pulpit.

It is better to be frightened into heaven

than lulled into hell.

*O*n a sin he hadn't experienced:

I don't have to eat swill

to preach on hogs.

On preaching to someone:
I don't have anyone in particular in mind.

I'm just shooting down the hole.
If you're down in it, I can't help it.

Plastic preachers produce
counterfeit Christians.

On the donkey that carried Jesus:

People **hardly noticed** the donkey;
they looked at Jesus.
So they cheered for Christ and not the donkey.
The preacher needs to be like a donkey,
but what a privilege!

The most **valuable contribution**
a preacher can make
is not when he is before his people
talking about God,
but when he is before God
talking about his people.

I'm a
nobody
telling
everybody
about
Somebody
Who can
save
anybody.

The test of my preaching is,

"Are others becoming more like Jesus?"

To young preachers:

Be prepared
to spend the rest of your life at your church,
or be prepared
to leave in the next fifteen minutes.

The same sermon that
comforts the afflicted
can afflict the comfortable.

PROPHECY

*I've stopped looking
for the signs
and started listening
for the shout.*

As the end gets *closer*, the day gets *darker*.
As the day gets *darker*, the saints shine *brighter*.
As the saints shine *brighter*, the world sees *clearer*.

Anybody can take a newspaper with
one hand and the Bible with the other hand
and see how everything—all history—is fitting into
the sockets of prophecy.

On the *Rapture*:
Cut my shoelaces; I'm ready to go.

Don't keep your head in the clouds of
prophecy.
Put your feet on the pavement of
soul winning.

On fulfilled prophecy:

Jesus is not looking backward quoting poetry.
David, by inspiration, was looking forward
and quoting Jesus.

On the return of Christ:

I don't want to be on the Program Committee;
I want to be on the Welcome Committee.

It seems to me that at this point in time we should be more concerned with the destiny of the species rather than the origin of the species.

Praise God!

It is growing gloriously dark.

And before long our Morning Star will appear.

The Jesus Christ is coming.

I wouldn't give up Christ
for twenty-four hours
or a million dollars
because Christ might come back in
those twenty-four hours and because I
wouldn't deny my Lord for all the
money in the world.

*P*ROPHECY

Even now the raging waters of God's wrath are
furiously pounding
against the dam of His mercy.
And one of these days,
the dam of God's mercy
will give way to God's judgment,
and the day of the Lord will come.

Waiting on the Lord
is like waiting for the sun to come up.
You can't hurry it. You can't stop it.
God is going to bring a sunrise to your soul.
Just wait for it and trust Him while you wait.

*W*e have a lot of soothsayers,

prognosticators,

and astrologers today—

a lot of so-called prophets.

But they're not prophetic;

they're pathetic.

What is this world
coming to?
It's coming to
Jesus!

P ROPHECY

*S*ALVATION

*C*ome
to
Jesus!

A man will go to hell unsaved, but he will never go unloved.

I promise you on the authority of the Word of God if you will trust Christ as your personal Savior, He will save you. If you can show me any time, any place, or anywhere that someone came to Jesus Christ in sincere repentance and faith and Jesus did not save that person, I'll close this Book and never preach from it again.

God put a cross between you and hell.
If you want to go to hell, you will have to
crawl over the cross of Jesus.

Christianity is not do—but DONE!

Life is too short.
Eternity is too long.
Souls are too precious.
The Gospel is too wonderful
for us to sleep through it all.

$\mathcal{D}$on't get the idea that Jesus died to save you from hell. He died to save you from sin. And if He can't save you from sin, He can't save you from hell.

$\mathcal{E}$ternal life is not something you get when you die; it's something you get when you believe.

$\mathcal{H}$eaven is not a reward for the righteous; it's a gift for the guilty.

Most people today are just interested in
making the world *a better place*

... to go to hell from.

Thank You for saving me, Jesus.
I receive it by faith.
I don't look for a sign.
I don't ask for a feeling.
I stand on Your Word.
And that settles it!

Sometimes I almost wish I were lost
so I could get saved all over again!

There are those who can preach the Gospel better than I can, but there is nobody who can preach a better Gospel than I can.

The worst form of badness is human goodness when human goodness becomes a substitute for the new birth.

You're free to choose.
You're not free not to choose.
And you're not free to choose the consequences of your choices. Your choices choose for you.

$\mathscr{T}$here is *no* omission in the Great Commission.

There is no one so bad he
cannot be saved and no one so good he
need not be saved.

We will be judged
not for *the sins that we have committed*
but for *the Light we have rejected.*

When you get to where you're going,
where will you be?

You're not going to heaven
by being baptized.
You could be baptized so many times the
tadpoles have your Social Security number
and still not go to heaven.

Be fishers of men...
You catch 'em, He'll clean 'em.

Evangelism is one beggar telling another beggar where to find bread.

THE GOSPEL is simply glorious and gloriously simple.

I'd like to ask what right any man has to call himself a follower of Jesus Christ if he is not a soul winner.

—R.A. Torrey

Suppose I just wrapped myself around a piece of apple pie. And you come to me and say, **"There's no such thing** as an apple pie. **I don't believe in** apple pie. And if there is apple pie, it is not good." I want to tell you, in spite of your arguments, I have the witness within me. **A Christian with a testimony** is never at the mercy of **an unbeliever with an argument** because the Christian has the **witness in himself.**

*We don't change the message;
the message changes us.*

The only thing between sinning man and judgment is time.

No matter how *faithfully* you attend church, how *generously* you give, how *circumspectly* you walk, how *eloquently* you teach, or how *beautifully* you sing—if you are not endeavoring to bring people to Jesus Christ, you are not right with God.

The Spirit is received;
joy is achieved;
the Gospel is believed.

Salvation

Calvary:

Earth's greatest tragedy,

heaven's greatest triumph.

God did not spare
His own Son from
the cross. What makes you
think He will spare you
from rejecting the
cross?

For a multitude of sins
there is a multitude of mercies.

God *thought* it.
Satan *fought* it.
Jesus *bought* it.
Grace *wrought* it.
Paul *taught* it.

I want to meet Jesus face-to-face,

Whom I've known heart to heart.

Baptism, whether a spoonful
or a tankful,
can never save anybody.
You are saved by
trusting Jesus.

Faith in faith
is just positive thinking,
but faith in Jesus
is salvation.

If you can have it and not know it,
you can lose it and not miss it.

If you were baptized before you were saved,
dear friend,
that is like having your funeral before you die.

*I*f you are not sealed by the Spirit, you will be
branded by the beast.

If we could know God in some way other than
faith, the smart guys would have a
head start.

If you are not *saved* by the Word,
you will be *judged* by the Word.

*J*esus didn't die to make bad people good,
but to make dead people live.

Jesus didn't come to make you a nicer person.
He came to radically,

dramatically,

and eternally

transform you.

*I*t's not a good heart we need,
but a new heart.

Salvation may be free to you and me,
but it *cost* the Lord Jesus *everything*.

It will be a great day in any land when people
stop enduring religion
and start enjoying salvation.

I'm not against education,
but you don't
come to God head first;
you come heart first.

Life is short. Death is sure.

Sin the curse, Christ the cure.

Hell is hot. Heaven is sweet.

Sin is black, Judgment pure.

Jesus saves.

Nobody is saved by keeping

the Ten Commandments.

If he could be,

Jesus Christ need never have died.

On not being able to lose your salvation:

God will clean house, but He won't move out.

Nature *forms* us;

    sin *deforms* us;

        school *informs* us;

            and prison *reforms* us.

    But only Christ *transforms* us.

*J*esus doesn't show us

the way to heaven.

He is the way to heaven.

*O*n not pleading for someone's salvation:

Anything I can talk you into,

someone else can talk you out of.

*S*ALVATION

349

On the age of accountability:
If you are old enough to know
what I'm talking about, you're old enough.

On salvation by works:
I wouldn't trust the
best fifteen minutes I
ever lived to get me
into heaven.

People aren't saved by our lives
but by His death.

ADRIANISMS

Put your faith where God has put your sins,
on Jesus.

Repent today.
Tomorrow you will have more sin to repent of
and less time to repent in.

Repentance
made in the time of storm
may sometimes
mean nothing in the still waters.

Salvation
doesn't come from following the life of Christ
but receiving the death of Christ.

Until you come to the end of you,
you won't come to the
beginning of Him.

Salvation
is not a plan;
it's a Man.

Salvation is not rooted in
the merit of man
but in the
mercy of God.

If God's love doesn't bring repentance,
God's judgment brings rebellion.

Some believe we have security only after we arrive in
heaven. But, wait a minute, the angels fell from heaven.
If we are not secure here, we are not secure there.
Security is not in a place, but a Person—Jesus.

The assurance of my salvation
comes not from the fact that I did trust Christ
but that I am trusting Christ for my salvation.

To be *almost* saved

is to be *totally* lost.

Some people are going to go to hell with a chest full of Sunday school attendance pins who have never received the Lord Jesus Christ. They have religion, but they don't have righteousness. They have culture, but they don't have Christ.

$\mathcal{S}$alvation is not getting
man out of Earth and into heaven.
It's getting
God out of heaven and into man.

$\mathcal{W}$e cannot receive
what He gives
unless we receive
Who He is.

If you come swaggering to God as a prince,
you'll go away as a beggar.

But if you come as a beggar,
you will go away as a prince.

$\mathcal{S}$ALVATION

You can *laugh* your way *into* hell
but not out.

*W*e're not to believe
something: we're to
receive **Someone**.

*W*hen we fish for **fish**, we take them out of a
beautiful life to **death**.
But when we fish for **men**, we take them out of
death to beautiful **life**.

Works never get us to heaven;
they just follow us to heaven.

The key to determining how much *something is worth* is how much *someone will pay* for it. That makes me want to shout because Jesus thought I was worth so much that He gave His life for me.

What Jesus does with you
will depend
on what you do with Him.

Adages and Axioms

When you learn that
Jesus is all you have,
you'll learn that
Jesus is enough.

We have **"In God We Trust"**
engraved on our money,

but we have **"Me First"**
written on our hearts.

The *Bible* is not a rule book;
the Bible is a *guidebook.*

The *Bible* is not a book of minute laws;
it's *a book of great principles.*

There is no problem that cannot be solved by prayer.

There are no problems too big to solve,

just people too small to solve them.

I believe all of life you can, more or less, divide into three categories. There are

    the beater-uppers,

       the passer-uppers,

         and the picker-uppers.

When someone becomes a Christian,

it is a supernatural transformation.

It is not like a tadpole becoming a frog.

It is a frog becoming a prince

by the kiss of grace.

How can we develop faith?

Be saturated in the Word,

be separated from sin,

be dedicated to the Son,

and be activated by the Spirit.

When you believe the **Bible**,

it is not a leap into the dark,

it is a step into the light.

Adrian, do you ever have any problems?

Only when I'm asleep

or awake.

We just have to keep on preaching
over and over again:
The Book—God's holy Word.
The blood—the atonement of the Lord Jesus.
The birth—a twice-born person.
The blessed hope—Jesus
is actually,
literally,
visibly,
bodily
coming back to this earth
one of these days.

THE BIBLE is:

Saving to the sinner;
Sweet to the saint;
Sufficient to the sufferer;
Satisfying to the scholar.

You never know the **ripple** that will touch the shore of **eternity** when you drop that stone of **grace** into somebody's **heart**.

Grace is God's acceptance of us.
Faith is our acceptance of God's acceptance of us.

The will of God for my life is
Jesus living His life through me—
nothing more,
nothing less,
nothing else.

Satan has leveled
all of the artillery of hell
at the home.

To ridicule a preacher who warns of hell
would be the same as
to ridicule a doctor who warns of cancer.

What should we do?
Pray for revival. Plan for survival.
Look for His arrival.

There are two books in the Bible that
would be good for you to visit every morning.

One is *Proverbs*,
and one is *Psalms*.

One teaches you how to *live*.
The other teaches you how to *worship*.

To worship
is your greatest need.

To worship
is your ultimate privilege.

To worship
is your supreme duty.

Nobody's happy all the time.
You're not expected to be.
But you're to have JOY all the time.
The Bible says, "Rejoice in the Lord always:
and again I say, Rejoice."

To take Jesus Christ out of Christianity
is like taking
the water out of a well,
the blue out of the sky,
notes out of music,
and numbers out of mathematics.
I'm telling you, folks,
Christianity is Christ.

A light that does not shine,
a spring that does not flow,
a seed that does not grow
is no more strange than
a life in Christ that does not witness.

Counseling is just loving people
and knowing God...
and getting the two together.

People say the church is full of hypocrites.
I'd rather spend some of the time
here on earth with some of the hypocrites
than eternity in hell with all of them.

It's better to have a Father
Who owns a bakery
than to have a warehouse
full of bread.

In college, I had a sign on my desk that said,

"He who would **not fall down**
ought not to walk in **slippery places."**

If you're having
trouble with faith,
try repentance.

JESUS is all you need.
You should seek nothing more
and settle for nothing less.

Prophecy is not given primarily
to tell you what the future holds.
It is given
to tell you who holds the future—*Jesus*.

*I*f your life is dull and insipid,

perhaps you ought to do

what Abraham did: Live by faith

and that'll turn the

monotonous to the momentous.

I don't have a failure
except a prayer failure.
I don't have a need
that prayer won't resolve.
There is not a temptation or a sin
that prayer won't resolve.
There is nothing
that is outside the realm of prayer.

I believe the reason we have so much
so-called "hell" in our world is
because we have so little in our pulpits.

If you're **not** absolutely certain
that you're **saved**, I want you to
pray this prayer:

"Dear God, I know that You love me, and I know that You want to save me. Jesus, You died to save me. You promised to save me if I would trust You. I do trust You. By faith I receive You as my Lord and Savior. Forgive my sin. Cleanse me. Save me, Lord Jesus.

Thank You for doing it. I receive it by faith like a child, and that settles it. Now begin to make me the person You want me to be, and help me, Lord Jesus, never to be ashamed of You. In Your name I pray. Amen."

ADRIANISMS

Dr. Adrian Rogers

Dr. Adrian Rogers, one of America's most respected Bible teachers, faithfully preached the Word of God for fifty-three years—thirty-two of those years as senior pastor of the historic Bellevue Baptist Church near Memphis, Tennessee.

He wrote eighteen books and over fifty booklets giving strength and encouragement on subjects such as marriage, prophecy, evangelism, and the Christian walk.

In 1987 he founded Love Worth Finding Ministries to communicate the glorious Gospel of Jesus Christ with millions around the world. The message of God's love continues today, and as he so aptly put it, "Truly, the sun never sets on the ministry of Love Worth Finding."

CPSIA information can be obtained
at www.ICGtesting.com
Printed in the USA
LVHW020302140819
627556LV00001B/1